TOLSTOI
THE LAW OF LOVE AND
LAW OF VIOLENCE

DATE DUE

D1112485

THE LAW OF LOVE
AND THE
LAW OF VIOLENCE

THE LAW OF LOVE AND THE LAW OF VIOLENCE

LEO TOLSTOY

Translated by Mary Koutouzow Tolstoy
With a Foreword by Baroness Budberg

HOLT, RINEHART AND WINSTON
New York   Chicago   San Francisco

Library of Congress Catalog Card Number: 72–108668
First Edition

Designer: Berry Eitel
SBN: 03–084531-x
Printed in the United States of America

FOREWORD

TOLSTOY'S wife is quoted to have said: "I lived with Leo Tolstoy for forty-eight years and I still do not know what sort of man he was."

This work, *The Law of Love and the Law of Violence*, among the last he ever wrote and known to very few, illustrates the imponderable quality of his genius. It is in the main line of his thinking but at the same time has a purity, a single-mindedness which you do not find in his other works, being a deliverance from the conflicting emotions that forever assailed this great, this never-to-be-repeated man.

It contains many quotations from what is here called the "Daily Reader," but which was entitled by him "Thoughts of Wise Men for Every Day." In a preface to this kind of diary he wrote: "Throughout the centuries the *best*, that is, the *real* people used to think about *it*." *It* is that about which he himself thought all his life even when he was passionately involved with other ideas. *It* is "how it will all end," about "what you have to seek for, seek relentlessly, all the time." Which is why the final appeal of this book to the young will be something the young of to-day must finally recognize for themselves.

Remarkable in everything, Tolstoy was remarkable in the insistence with which he began to talk "about *it*" from his early days and in later years with an obsessional uniformity such as sometimes is to be found in the lives of saints or in the case histories of the mentally deranged. The book is repetitive, yes, but so are the ancient holy books of India, the Upanishads, the Bhagavad Gita, the books of the Jewish prophets, the teachings of Christ and Buddha, and the Koran.

Sir Isaiah Berlin wrote *The Hedgehog and the Fox* whose title is taken from a line by a Greek poet: "The fox knows many things, but the hedgehog knows one big thing," and then proceeds to divide the great thinkers and writers of the world into the two categories. Dante is in the first, Shakespeare in the second. Plato, Pascal, Hegel, Dostoevsky, Nietzsche, Ibsen, Proust are, according to him, hedgehogs; Aristotle, Montaigne, Molière, Goethe, Pushkin, Balzac, are foxes.

Which is Tolstoy? Why is it such a problem to define him? Berlin proposes that he was by nature a fox but believed himself to be a hedgehog. Well, in my opinion, he was undoubtedly a hedgehog. He knew unerringly *one* big thing of which this book provides perhaps the most complete expression: Love and not violence should govern all our actions in this world.

BARONESS BUDBERG

September 1969

THE LAW OF LOVE
AND THE
LAW OF VIOLENCE

NOTE

THIS work of Leo Tolstoy's was not published in its entirety in Russia at the time it was written. Some parts of it, with many omissions owing to censorship, came out in issues of the *Kiev Bulletin* in February 1909. It was subsequently published in Russian in England by the Free Age Press, Christchurch, in July 1909, and then in 1917 in a periodical called *The Soldier Citizen* under the editorship of Vladimir Tchertkoff. It has since reappeared in the Soviet Union in the complete edition of Tolstoy's works published in 1956.

Meanwhile a friend of Tolstoy's, Halpérine-Kaminsky, translated the work into French from the manuscript, and published it in France. Shortly after this Paul Bourget's drama *La Barricade* was produced in Paris. This play, based on the idea of inter-class warfare, was the subject of much controversy. Halpérine-Kaminsky sent Tolstoy criticisms of the play and received the following reply:

My Dear Halpérine-Kaminsky,

Thank you very much for the articles on "The Barricade." I read the most interesting ones at once.

Note

Yes, it is a very significant phenomenon, and I should like to give you my opinion on this subject. But I have so little strength left, and so short a time to live, and so much work on hand, that I doubt if I shall entirely realize my desire.

For the moment, what struck me most in the debates caused by Mr. Bourget's play is their astonishing mixture of profound erudition, great intelligence, extraordinary elegance of language, and subtle courtesy towards the adversary; but also the most brutal selfishness, concerned only with personal and class interests, and absolute ignorance of religious and moral principles, even those that are indispensable to our lives, and without which man descends to the level of the beasts; in spite of the invention of marvellous flying machines, or of the wonderful perfection of the artists of the Théâtre Français, of the Vaudeville, etc.

I am particularly surprised that men like M. Bourget and his friends can still speak so seriously of Catholicism in France in 1910, after Voltaire, Rousseau, and many other thinkers. Nothing proves more clearly how misguided these men have become; not as to their intelligence but as to their reasoning; not as to their polish and brilliancy, but as to their morality. In this conflict it is evident that *tous les moyens sont bons.*

We know well, they say, that Catholicism is the most vulgar, the most absurd, and the most stupifying of lies, and that it has long since been denounced and stripped bare; but it serves our purposes: let us make use of it . . .

My best wishes,
LEO TOLSTOY

PREFACE

The light is come into the world, and men loved the darkness rather than the light; for their works were evil. For every one that doeth evil hateth the light, and cometh not to the light, lest his works should be reproved. But he that doeth the truth cometh to the light, that his works may be made manifest, that they have been wrought in God.

(John, iii, 19–21.)

The worst thing of all is when man begins to fear the truth lest it denounce him.

(Blaise Pascal.)

The glory of the good is in their conscience and not in the mouths of men.[1]

THE only reason why I am writing this is because, knowing the one means of salvation for Christian humanity, from its physical suffering as well as from the moral corruption in which it is sunk, I, who am on the edge of the grave, cannot be silent.

All thinking people must realize that the present life of Christian nations will deteriorate more and

---

[1] The epigraphs placed at the beginning of the chapters, and not signed, are quotations from Tolstoy's works, made by the author himself. (Translator's note.)

ix

more if we do not determine to change it. The misery of the disinherited and the luxury of the rich increase each day; the struggle of all against all—revolutionaries against governments, governments against revolutionaries, oppressed nations against their oppressors, state against state, the West against the East—is becoming more and more bitter.

Many are aware of this; unfortunately they very rarely see the cause of this pitiful situation, and still less the means for remedying it. They give all sorts of reasons and propose numerous remedies, but not the only one which is right.

The cause of the unhappy situation of Christian humanity is the lack of a superior view of life and a rule of conduct in accordance with it, a rule to be held in common by all people professing Christianity.

The cure for this situation, a cure neither fantastic nor artificial, but natural, can be found in the practical observance of the view of life revealed to humanity nineteen centuries ago, and which answers to-day to its intellectual and moral development; that is to say, *the Christian Doctrine in its true sense.*

THE LAW OF LOVE
AND THE
LAW OF VIOLENCE

 I

*One of the most vulgar of all prejudices is that of the clever
who believe that one can live without faith.*
(*Daily Reading*, 2nd Part, Introduction.)[1]

*True religion consists in establishing the relation of each of
us towards the infinite life that surrounds us, the life that
unites us to the infinite, and guides us in all our acts.*
(*Daily Reading*, 2nd Part, 1, 2.)

*If you feel that you no longer have faith, you should know that
you are in the most dangerous situation in which a man can
find himself on earth.*

MEN live in a reasonable way and on good
terms with each other when they are united
by the same understanding of life; that is to say,

---

[1] The work entitled *Daily Reading*, from which many epigraphs
are taken, was written by Tolstoy with quotations from his own
writings, and from those of great writers of all countries and all
times.

by a religion that satisfies all of them alike and gives them the same model of conduct. But when it happens that their view of life as a result of moral and intellectual progress becomes more precise and requires a new model of conduct, while men continue to follow the old one, their lives become unhappy and they no longer live in harmony.

The evil is aggravated more and more as men continue to ignore the new religious ideas and the ethic which derives from them, and observe instead the model imposed by the old. Instead of acknowledging a religious viewpoint corresponding to their phase of development, they imagine one that justifies their way of living, but nevertheless does not answer to the moral needs of the majority of mankind.

This phenomenon has occurred several times in the history of humanity; but never, I believe, has the discord between the mode of life of our societies and the religious ideals they have formally adopted been so great: they continue to live a life which is in effect pagan.

In my opinion this disagreement is so marked because the Christian view of life at the moment of its formation went far beyond the moral and intellectual level of the peoples who acknowledged it at that time. That is why the code of conduct which it recommended was too greatly opposed not only to the habits of individual people but to the whole social organization of pagans, who had become Christians in name only.

Thus it is that these peoples became attached to a false Christianity, represented by the Church, whose principles differ from those of paganism only in a lack of sincerity. For that very reason faith in the Christian doctrines has disappeared little by little without being replaced by any other. That is why the Christian world has come to its present condition: the majority of its adherents possess no explanation of the meaning of life, that is to say, no religion and no common code of conduct.

3 < The working masses, even though they outwardly profess the religion of the Church, do not believe in it any more, do not practise it in their daily lives and only follow its traditions for reasons of habit or propriety. As for the so-called cultivated classes, they either no longer believe positively in anything at all, or they pretend to believe in the Christianity of the Church for political reasons; or else a small minority believes sincerely in the Christian doctrines, contrary to the life it actually leads, and seeks to justify its belief by all sorts of insidious sophistries. That is the sole reason for the unhappy condition in which Christianity now finds itself.

Things are complicated still more by the fact that because of its long duration, some of our leaders for whom this unbelief is profitable pretend to believe what they do not believe at all; others, our intellectuals, who are the more corrupt, openly preach the uselessness for men of our time of such a conception of life, or faith, and the rules of conduct that result from it, and try to make men believe that the sole fundamental law of human life is the struggle for existence, which requires us to be guided purely by our passions or our natural needs.

The regrettable cause of all our miseries is, therefore, this unconscious lack of faith of the masses and the conscious ignoring of the necessity for religion by the so-called cultivated classes.

*Man has an irresistible tendency to believe that no one sees
him when he himself does not see: like children who close
their eyes so they may be invisible.*

(Lichtenberg.)

*Men of our time believe that all the insanity and cruelty
of our lives, the ridiculous wealth of a few, the envious
poverty of the majority, wars and all forms of violence,
are perceived by nobody, and that nothing prevents us from
continuing to live thus.*

*Error continues to be no less erroneous merely because
accepted by the majority.*

(*Daily Reading,* 6–ix, 7, 8, and the conclusion.)

HAVING accepted the Christian doctrine in the
form corrupted by the Church, the pagans,
satisfied at first with this new doctrine, withdrew
little by little from the Christianity of the Church,
and ended by living without any religious view of
life and the rules of conduct resulting from it.

As the majority of men are unable to live without
a common code of conduct, life, as I have said,
gradually becomes unhappier. It will not be able to
continue to hold good in its present form.

Farm labourers, dispossessed of the land, and

consequently of the possibility of enjoying the fruit of their labour, hate the landed proprietors and capitalists who enslave them. The proprietors and the capitalists, knowing the sentiments they inspire in the workers, distrust them, fear them, and seek to keep them in submission by the organized force of government. Thus it is that the situation of the workers becomes steadily worse and their dependence upon the rich grows; while the wealth of the rich, their power over the workers, their fear and their hate, continues to increase.

This is equally the cause of the progressive increase in the arming of nation against nation, of the expenditure in military preparation on land, sea and in the air; preparations having as their sole end international carnage. And these murders are committed because all Christian people (not individuals, but people united into States) hate each other and are ready at any moment to hurl themselves at each other in war.

Thus it is that each great power, by observing antiquated patriotic traditions, oppresses one or several groups of people and forces them to participate in the life of the dominating nation that they hate, for example: Austria, Prussia, England, Russia, France, oppress Poland, Ireland, India, Finland, the Caucasus, Algeria, etc. So, apart from the hatred of the poor and the rich, and of independent States for each other, the hatred of oppressed nations for their oppressors spreads and develops.

The tragedy is that all these hatreds, so contrary to human nature, are not condemned as vices, but on the contrary are exalted and raised to the level of virtues. The hatred of the oppressed workers for the rich is commended in the same style as the love of liberty, fraternity and equality. The hatred of Germans for French, English for Americans, Russians for Japanese, and vice versa, is considered a patriotic virtue. The hatred of Poles for Russians and Prussians, Prussians and Russians for Poles and Finns, is reciprocated and exalted even more.

But the plagues to which I have drawn attention are not sufficient to demonstrate the impossibility of continuing in our present direction. If our world possessed a rule of religious conduct, we could look upon the evils that inflict it as transient, occasional phenomena. In reality, the religion which we see professed, that of the Church, is a mendacious one. There are several forms of it, Catholic, Orthodox, Protestant, etc., and all are in a state of permanent hostility. There exists also a false science, equally divided, whose denominations are equally quarrelsome. There are lies—political, international, partisan; lies of artifice, lies of tradition and habit, lies of all sorts, but no rule of moral conduct imposed by a proper view of life.

The men of the Christian world lead the existence of beasts, and take their selfish interests as their guide, and are in a state of perpetual struggle among themselves. What distinguishes them from the beasts is the constancy of an animal's needs—for food and claws and other means of survival and defence; while men pass with vertiginous haste from roads to railroads, from animal locomotion to steam, from the spoken and written word to printing, to the telegraph, the telephone; from sailing vessels to transatlantic liners, from clean armaments to cannon, machine guns, bombs, and military aeroplanes. It is our agitated life that is getting madder and madder, unhappier and unhappier, because men, instead of keeping to a spiritual, moral principle that would unite them in a society of peace and concord, are guided by animal instincts for which they seek to achieve satisfaction by trading on their intellectual faculties.

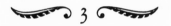 3

*But whoso shall cause one of these little ones that believe on
me to stumble, it is better for him that a great millstone
should be hanged about his neck, and that he should be sunk
in the depth of the sea.*

(Matthew, xviii, 6, 7.)

*One cannot struggle against the calls of conscience: these
calls come from God; that is why it is preferable to answer
them at once.*

(*Daily Reading*, October 23rd.)

*The evil committed by man not only weakens his soul and
deprives him of true happiness, but more often than not
falls back on the one who commits it.*

(*Daily Reading*, June 6th.)

THE majority of the men of our time, seeing the
constant increase of their misfortunes, employ
the only means of salvation that according to their
lights they consider rational: the oppression of some
by others.

Those who see their interest in the maintenance
of the existing regime defend it with the force that
the State puts at their command: those who wish
to change the present order of things equally resort

to violence in order to replace it by a new one they believe to be better.

One cannot count any longer the number of revolutions and counter revolutions in the history of the Christian world. But however much the social forms are modified as a result their basis remains the same. The domination of the many by the few, corruption, lies, the fear of the oppressor in face of the oppressed, servitude, anger and the brutalizing of the masses, all these things remain as they were, and even spread and develop further.

What is going on now in Russia, in particular, throws into evident relief not only the futility but the harmful effect of using violence as a means of ensuring social cohesion.

The incidents, so frequent a short time ago, of highway robbery, the assassination of policemen, officers and agents, attacks on high functionaries, are becoming rarer every day, while death sentences and executions are increasing. For the past two years they have not stopped shooting and hanging people, and those executed can be counted by thousands. Thousands also have been killed by revolutionary bombs. But since the number of those killed by the regime is incomparably greater than those killed by revolutionaries, the former triumphs and believes it has won. It does not doubt that it will be able to continue in existence through maintaining lies by means of violence, and violence by means of lies.

The mistake of all political doctrines, from the

most conservative to the most advanced, which has brought men to their present pitiful condition, is the same: the belief that it is possible to keep men social by means of violence so as to make them accept their present organizations and the rule of conduct they impose.

Certainly, it is possible to push a man forcibly in the direction that he refuses to take. It is thus that animals behave, as well as men led on only by their passions. It is natural and comprehensible. But how shall one understand the reasoning by which violence is a means of inviting men to do everything we wish them to do?

Constraint always consists in forcing others, by threats of suffering or death, to do what they refuse to do. But they act against their own wishes only so long as they consider themselves weaker than their oppressors. From the moment that they feel themselves stronger they will not only cease to obey, but, incensed by the struggle and by all that they have suffered, they will first regain their liberty, and then in their turn impose their will upon those who disagree with them. From which it should be quite evident that the struggle between oppressors and oppressed, far from constituting a means of social organization, leads to disorder and total discord.

It is so obvious that it would be superfluous to speak of it, if the lie, according to which violence is a means of social cohesion, had not been implanted for so long a time, and was not admitted by tacit consent to be an indisputable truth, as much by those who profit by it as by the majority of those who are its victims.

This lie existed before the Christian era, and has since survived in all its strength. The only difference between former times and our own is that formerly it was hidden from men, while to-day the truth of Christ, according to which violence is only a means of disunion, stands out more and more clearly. The moment that men understand this truth they will no longer be able to endure violence without revolting against it.

This is observed to-day among the oppressed in every country. Not only are they beginning to perceive this truth but the oppressors in their turn are becoming aware of it. They are no longer so certain they are acting well and justly when they use violence towards the weak. Accustomed to their reciprocal situations, the leaders and the led are seeking to persuade each other by arguments, mostly false, that brute force is necessary and useful; but they feel already deep within themselves that their acts of cruelty, instead of gaining them their desired goal draw them further away from it.

 4

When, among a hundred men one man dominates ninety-nine, it is iniquity, it is despotism; when ten dominate ninety, it is injustice, it is oligarchy; when fifty-one dominate forty-nine (and this only theoretically, for, in reality, among these fifty-one there are ten or eleven masters), then it is justice, then it is liberty.

Could one imagine anything more ridiculous, more absurd, than this reasoning? However, this is the very one that serves as a basic principle for everyone who extols better social conditions.

All the nations in the world are restless. An active force that seems to be preparing the way for a cataclysm is felt everywhere. Man has never assumed so great a responsibility. Each moment brings troubles that become more and more absorbing. One has the impression that something great is going to be accomplished. But on the eve of the appearance of Christ the world was then also expecting great events; yet it did not welcome Him when He came. In the same way the world might feel birth pangs before His next coming and go on failing to understand what is happening.
(Lucie Malaury. *Daily Reading,* June 30th.)

And be not afraid of them that kill the body, but are not able to kill the soul: but rather fear him who is able to destroy both soul and body in Hell.
(Matthew, x, 28.)

THE states of the Christian world have not only reached, but in our day have passed the limits towards which the states of ancient times were approaching before their dismemberment. We can see this from the fact that each step we make to-day towards material progress not only does not advance us towards the general well-being, but shows us, on the contrary, that all these technical improvements only increase our miseries. One can imagine other machines, submarine, subterranean and aerial, for transporting men with the rapidity of lightning; one could multiply to infinity the means of propagating human speech and thought, but it would remain no less the case that these travellers, so comfortably and rapidly transported, are neither willing nor able to commit anything but evil, and the thoughts and words they pour forth would only incite men to further harm. As to the beautifully perfected armaments of destruction, which, while diminishing the risk of those who employ them, make carnage easier, they only give further proof of the impossibility of persevering in the direction we are going.

Thus, the horror of the situation of the Christian world has a double aspect: on the one hand the absence of a moral principle of union and on the other a gradual lowering of man to a degree below that of the animals; in spite of his intellectual progress and the complexity of the lies that hide from us our misery and our cruelty.

The lies cover the cruelty, the cruelty causes the

spreading of the lies, and both increase like insidious snow balls. But everything must come to an end. And I believe that a crisis in this horrible situation is approaching. The evils, resulting from the lack of a religious ideal corresponding to our epoch, are the inevitable conditions of progress; they should as inevitably disappear after the adoption of such an ideal.

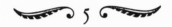

From the day when the first members of councils placed exterior authority higher than interior, that is to say, recognized the decisions of men united in councils as more important and more sacred than reason and conscience; on that day began the deceit that has caused the loss of millions of human beings and which continues its disastrous work to the present day.

In 1682 the English doctor Laitan, an honourable man, having written a book against the bishopric, was judged and condemned to the following punishment: he was cruelly whipped, one ear was cut off, his nose was split, and the initials of the words Trouble Maker were marked on one cheek with a hot iron. Seven days later he was again whipped, although the wounds of his former punishment were not yet healed; the other side of his nose was split, his other ear cut off, and his other cheek marked. All this was done in the name of Christian charity.

(Maurice Davidson.)

Christ founded no church, established no State, made no laws, imposed no government or exterior authority; he simply set himself to write the law of God in the hearts of men in order that they might be able to govern themselves.

(Herbert Newton.)

17

THE special characteristic of the situation in which the Christian world finds itself to-day is that its social organization is founded on a doctrine which, if it were truly accepted, would destroy the existing regime; and that the possibility of this acceptance, obscure up till now, is beginning to become apparent.

One might compare our social organization to a house built, not even on sand, but on ice. And its foundation is melting, and the house is beginning to fall in.

As long as the majority of the faithful, deceived by the Church, had only a rudimentary idea of the doctrine of Christ, and in the place of former fetiches adored Christ-God, his mother, the saints, the relics; as long as they believed in miracles, in the Holy Sacrament, in the Redemption, in the infallibility of the princes of the Church, the pagan organization of life could keep going and give every satisfaction to believers. They could accept in the same way the meaning of life that the Church gives them and the rule of conduct that resulted from it.

Unhappily for the faith imposed by the Church, there existed the Scriptures, that the Church itself recognized as holy. In spite of the efforts of the ecclesiastics to hide the true meaning of the evangelistic doctrine from the laity; in spite of having forbidden the Scriptures to be translated into the language of the people; in spite of their false interpretations, nothing could hide the light that filtered through the lies of the Church, and illuminated the souls of those whose eyes were opening more and more to the truth.

In proportion as education spread, as printing replaced writing, the Scriptures became more accessible, and men could not help but perceive the striking contradictions between the order of existing things upheld by the Church, and the evangelistic doctrine it acknowledged as holy. Read and understood exactly as they are, the Scriptures appeared as a frank and explicit denial of both the State and the Church.

In becoming more and more evident, this contradiction has resulted in loss of the faith imposed by the Church, and it is only by tradition, propriety, or fear that the majority of men continue to practise the outer forms of the Catholic, Orthodox or Protestant cults—but without believing in the inner truths of their religion.

I do not mention here the little communities that reject the ecclesiastic doctrines entirely and which profess their own doctrine, approaching more or less to true Christian teaching; the number of their adherents are too few in comparison with the enormous numbers of men who are becoming more and more devoid of any religious feeling at all. If the popular masses still practise the official cult outwardly, the upper classes, perceiving with still more precision the contradictions contained in the Church doctrine, turn away from it entirely. They cannot adopt the true doctrine of Christ, since this is in opposition to the existing state of affairs and would destroy altogether the privileges they enjoy.

So the immense majority of the Christian world practise the forms of the Church simply out of interest or decorum; while the minority not only do not acknowledge the existing religion, but influenced by what is called science, consider all religions as vestiges of superstition, and act only under the impulse of their instincts.

The peoples who accepted the Christian doctrine at the time when this doctrine was superior to their moral development are now fallen into a state of complete irreligion, their moral level being even lower than that of those professing much inferior, and even quite crude beliefs.

 6

*The corruption of Christianity takes us further away from
the establishment of the Kingdom of God on earth; but
Christian truth, like fires that smoulder in dry wood, has
consumed its covering and broken forth. The meaning of
Christianity has already been revealed to everyone, and its
effect is becoming greater than the falsehood that covers it.*

*I see a new religion, founded on confidence in man, calling
upon the unspoiled sentiments that are lying asleep in us,
believing that we can love good for itself without any idea
of recompense and that the divine principle is in us.*

(Solter.)

*What we require, what is necessary for the people, what our
time needs for us to be raised from the mud of egotism,
doubt and negativeness in which we are plunged, is faith;
thanks to it our souls will stop wandering in pursuit of
selfish ends and will be able to march in unison by acknowledging a single origin, a single law, a single end. Every
firm belief that rises from the ruins of former religions
modifies the order of existing things, for all strong beliefs
accompany every branch of human activity.*

*Humanity repeats in two different formulas and in differ-
ent degrees the words of the prayer: "Thy Kingdom come
on earth as it is in Heaven."*

(Mazzini.)

*One can neither weigh nor measure the evil that false
religion has caused and is still causing.*

*Religion is the establishment of the relation that exists
between man, God and the universe, and the definition of*

*man's mission that results from it. How miserable our
lives would be if this relation and this definition were false.*

*It is not sufficient to throw away the false religion, that is
to say, the false relation of man as regards the universe;
we have still to establish the true.*

(*Daily Reading*, September 19th.)

THE fact that one part of the pagan world
accepted a religious doctrine, which, far from
being at the moral level of the society of that time,
undermined its very base, has a certain tragedy
about it; but at the same time it constitutes the most
fortunate event that could have happened to nations
professing the Christian religion.

Presented to pagans in an unnatural form, this
doctrine appeared to them as a simple refinement
of their crude conception of the Divinity, as a higher
idea of the mission of man and of his moral needs.
But the real significance of the doctrine was so
hidden from them by the dogmas and practices of
the cult, that they did not even suspect it. And this
in spite of the precise teaching of Christ in the
Scriptures, which is acknowledged by the Church
as a divine revelation.

Happily this doctrine corresponds so well with
the spiritual nature of man, that in spite of the mass
of dogmas under which it is buried, those who have
greater intuition of the truth see through into its

real meaning and realize how it contradicts the existing order of things.

The fathers of the ancient church: Tatien, Clement, Origen, Tertullian, Cyprien, Lactance and others, had already realized this contradiction. It was the same in the Middle Ages. It has been revealed with particular force in modern times. And its recognition is shown by the appearance of a great number of religious sects, rejecting government that is contrary to the Christian doctrine condemning violence.

It has been equally recognized by the humanitarian teachings that claim to have nothing in common with Christianity, but which are really nothing else than partial manifestations of the Christian conscience; such are the socialist, Communist and anarchist beliefs.

The cause of the sufferings of Christian nations is thus the theoretical acceptance of a doctrine, which if applied, would inevitably abolish the order of things to which these nations are accustomed and which they do not wish to renounce.

Their great good fortune is in having admitted Christianity, which, even when falsified, still contains the truth. In fact, these nations to-day are being brought to the necessity of recognizing the true meaning of the doctrine which alone is able to save men from their present hopeless condition.

7

The principal cause of our bad social organization is false belief.

We ought to pay great attention to our public affairs; we should be ready to modify our opinions, to renounce our former ones, and to thoroughly understand the new. We should cast off our prejudices and should reason with an entirely free mind. The sailor who keeps the sail set in the same direction in spite of the changing of the wind will never reach port.

(Henry George.)

It is only necessary to adopt frankly the doctrine of Christ in order to perceive at once the horrible lie in which each and every one of us is living.

(*Daily Reading,* January.)

THE Christian doctrine, the real significance of which we are understanding more and more, teaches that man's mission is to manifest better and better the Principle of everything; and it is love that proves the presence of this Principle in us. That is why the highest law that should guide us is love.

The ancient religions all recognized love as an essential condition for a happy existence. The sages of Egypt, the Brahmans, the Stoics, the Buddhists, declared the principal virtues to be kindness, pity, compassion, and charity; in one word, love in all its forms. The highest of these doctrines, especially those of Buddha and of Lao-Tse, recommended love for all living things, and for people to return good for evil.

However, none of them put this virtue as a supreme law that should be the only motive for our acts. This was the distinctive feature of the most recent religion, that of Christ. All previous doctrines proclaimed the love of one's neighbour as one of the virtues; that of Christ sees in love the metaphysical principle behind everything, the supreme law that should guide us in our daily life and which admits of no exception whatever.

Christ's teaching should not be considered as entirely new, differing profoundly from former beliefs; it is only the clearer and more precise expression of the principle that previous religions divined and taught instinctively. Thus it is that instead of love being merely one of the virtues, as it was for them, Christianity has made it a supreme law, offering man an absolute rule of conduct. The Christian doctrine explains why this law is the highest, and indicates as well the acts that man should or should not commit after having acknowledged the truth of this teaching. It follows, with absolute clearness and precision, that the observance of the supreme law, because it is supreme, should not admit of any exception—as the previous doctrines did—and that love is only love when it is given in the same degree to aliens, to the adherents of other religions, and even to the enemies who hate us and do us harm.

That is the progress made by Christianity over previous religions, and there lies its principal virtue.

The explanation of why this commandment is the supreme law of life is given with special clearness in the Epistle of John:

> "Beloved, let us love one another: for love is of God; and every one that loveth is begotten of God, and knoweth God. He that loveth not knoweth not God; for God is love. No man hath beheld God at any time: if we love one another God abideth in us, and his love is perfected in us. God is love; and he that abideth in love abideth in God, and God abideth in him.
>
> "We know that we have passed out of death into life, because we love the brethren. He that loveth not abideth in death."
>
> (The First Epistle of John, iv, 7, 8, 12, 16; iii, 14.)

According to this doctrine our ego, our life, is the divine principle limited by our body, which manifests itself in us through love; which is why the true life of each of us is in the manifestation of love.

How we should interpret this conception of the law of love in our actions, is indicated to us in the Scriptures repeatedly and with a special clearness and precision in the fourth commandment of the Sermon on the Mount.

> "Ye have heard that it was said: An eye for an eye, and a tooth for a tooth (Exodus, 21, 14): but I say unto you, Resist not him that is evil."
>
> (Matthew, v, 38.)

Foreseeing, no doubt, the exceptions that would appear inevitable when the law of love is applied, the verses 39 and 40 of the same chapter state clearly that there are and cannot be any circumstances whatever permitting any deviation from the strict commandment of love: Do not do unto others what you would not have them do unto you.

> And it is said: "Whosoever smiteth thee on thy right cheek, turn to him the other also; and if any man would go to law with thee, and take away thy coat, let him have thy cloak also."

In other words, this means that violence directed against you can never justify the use of violence on your part.

The same condemnation of our breaking the law of love, when we try and justify it by the attitude of others, is even more clearly indicated in the last commandment of the Sermon on the Mount:

> "Ye have heard that it was said, Thou shall love thy neighbour, and hate thine enemy: (Lev. xix, 17, 18) but I say unto you, Love your enemies, and pray for them that persecute you; that ye may be sons of your father who is in Heaven; for he maketh his sun to rise on the evil

and the good, and sendeth rain on the just and unjust.
For if ye love them that love you, what reward have ye?
Do not even the publicans the same? Ye therefore shall
be perfect, as your heavenly Father is perfect."

(Matthew, v, 43–48.)

And it is this law of love and its recognition as a
rule of conduct in all our relations with friends,
enemies and offenders which must inevitably bring
about the complete transformation of the existing
order of things, not only among Christian nations,
but among all the peoples of the globe.

And this is the essential difference between the
Christian doctrine in its true conception and all previous religions; this is the progress that has been
accomplished in the universal conscience. The previous religious and moral doctrines that acknowledged the benefit of love in human life admitted
however certain circumstances in which the realization of this law cannot be obligatory. But, as soon
as it ceases to be an immovable law, its beneficence
disappears and the doctrine of love is reduced to
fruitless teaching, not modifying in any way the
mode of life that is founded on violence. By con-
trast, the true Christian doctrine, making of the law
of love a rule permitting no exceptions, in this way
rules out the possibility of any violence, and cannot
in consequence help but condemn all regimes which
are founded on it.

It is exactly this significance of Christianity that
was hidden from men by false Christianity, because

the latter acknowledges love not as a supreme law, but, in the manner of previous religions, only as *one* of the rules of conduct, to be usefully observed only when circumstances do not prevent it.

8

The disasters caused by wars and military preparations surpass in horror the motives that provoke them and which are held to justify them; but the motives themselves are most often ignored by the victims of war.

(*Daily Reading*, June 17th.)

Men are so accustomed to see order maintained by the aid of force, that they cannot imagine a social organization operating without constraints.

(*Daily Reading*, August 14th.)

If men were absolutely virtuous, they would never move an inch from the truth.

  The truth is only harmful to him who does evil. Whoever does good, loves truth.

(*Daily Reading*, August 29th.)

Reason is frequently the slave of sin; it strives to justify it.

(*Daily Reading*, August 29th.)

I am often astonished to see men defend certain strange maxims, whether religious, political or scientific. Seek further and you will find that he is only defending his own situation.

(*Daily Reading*, May 27th.)

THE true Christian doctrine consists only in the recognition of love as the *supreme law* of life, not admitting any exception. This means that the pretended Christian doctrine which does admit of exceptions such as the possibility of the use of violence in the enforcement of other laws, is a contradiction as obvious as cold fire or warm ice.

It would seem natural that if the possibility is once admitted that men may torture or kill their fellow beings in the name of humanity, others may claim the same right to torture and kill in the name of some ideal of the future. The admission of a single exception to the law of love destroys entirely its beneficial effect, although it is the basis of all religious or moral doctrines. This seems so self-evident that one is annoyed at being obliged to prove it; nevertheless, the believers or the non-believers of the Christian world—the latter acknowledging the moral law—look upon the idea of love condemning violence as fantastic and inapplicable to real life.

We can see that governments insist that good order cannot be maintained without violence, really meaning by the word "order" the maintenance of a regime that permits a minority to profit as much as it likes by the work of the majority. We can see why they say it, for the suppression of violence would take away the means of their survival and condemn their ancient injustices.

This ought not to be the case, it would seem, for the mass of workers who employ violence on each other and who suffer from it so cruelly. The situation of the oppressed should not be compared to the constraint used directly by the stronger on the weaker, or by a greater number on a smaller. Here, in effect, it is the minority who oppress the majority, thanks to a lie established ages ago by clever people, in virtue of which men despoil each other for small profit of comparably much greater advantages—such as liberty—and are exposed to much crueller suffering.

The origin of this lie was revealed four centuries ago by the French writer La Boetie, in his work, *Voluntary Slavery*. He said:

"It is not bands of horsemen, it is not companies of infantry, nor is it arms that defend the tyrant; but, and it will not at first be believed, true as it is, there are always four or five who control the tyrant, four or five who hold the country in servitude for him. There are always five or six who have the ear of the tyrant and access to him, and who have offered themselves, or are called upon by him, to be accomplices of his cruelty, the companions of his pleasure, panders to his lust, and sharers in his pillage. These six train their chief so well that he must be wicked not only on account of his own brutality, but of theirs also. These six have six hundred who profit under them and act towards them as the six act towards the tyrant. These six hundred have under them six thousand whom they have raised up and to whom they have given the government of provinces or the handling of taxes, that they may control

33

their avarice and cruelty. They perform their duties when it seems good to them, and do so much evil besides that they could not exist except under protection, nor be dispensed with except by means of law and punishment.

"Great are the consequences that result from this. And anyone who enjoyed looking closer into this net would see that not only the six thousand, but hundreds of thousands, millions, attach themselves to the tyrant by this cord; helping themselves by means of it, as, in Homer, Jupiter boasts that if he pulls a chain he will draw all the gods to him. From this came the rise of the senate, the establishment of new states and the election of offices, not certainly to reform justice, but to keep the tyrant in power.

"In sum, we owe our present condition to the favours, to the gains and advantages that one acquires from the tyrants, who find as many people to whom tyranny seems profitable, as those for whom liberty would be better. If physicians say there is something the matter with one part of our body, although the rest is quite well, they come at once to the infected part. In the same way, as soon as a king is declared a tyrant, all the wicked, all the dregs of the kingdom (I do not say a pile of robbers and cheats who can do very little evil or good in a republic, but those who are taxed with intense ambition and extraordinary avarice), gather around him and uphold him in order to share in the booty and to be petty tyrants under a greater one.

"Thus we have our great thieves and famous corsairs; some search out the country, others rob the travellers; some lie in ambush, others on watch; some assassinate, others do the robbing; and even here there are degrees of precedence, and while some are only servants, others are the chiefs, although one and all share in the booty or at least in the search for it. They say that the Sicilian pirates assembled in such great numbers that Pompey the Great had to be sent against them; but they allied themselves with several splendid cities and towns, in whose harbours they could hide with great security when they returned from their raids, and whom they recompensed with a certain percentage of their pillage.

"Thus the tyrant enslaved his subjects and was protected by those from whom, since they were worth nothing, he should himself have been protected; but, as they say, if one cuts wood, one makes wedges of the same kind of wood: so the archers, so the guards, so the halberdiers. Not that they do not suffer occasionally on his account: but these lost souls, these people abandoned by God and man, are content to endure evil in order to commit it in their turn, not on those who inflict it on them, but on those who suffer from it like themselves but are unable to perpetrate it further."

It would seem that the workers, not gaining any advantage from the restraint that is exercised on them, should at last realize the lie in which they are living and free themselves in the simplest and easiest way; by abstaining from taking part in the violence that is only possible with their co-operation.

It would be so simple and so natural to make the agricultural labourers, who are in the majority in Russia and other countries, understand that for centuries they have been suffering by their own default and without any advantage: that the exclusive possession of the land by those who do not work it is maintained by themselves, acting as guards, police agents and soldiers; that all the taxes are imposed by them, inasmuch as they are employed by the exchequer; and, when they have at last understood all this, to get them to say to those they consider their leaders:

"Leave us alone. If you, emperors, presidents, generals, judges, bishops, professors and other learned men, if you have need of armies, navies, ecclesiastical courts, prisons, gallows, guillotines, prepare them all yourselves; tax yourselves, judge yourselves, imprison and execute each other, exterminate yourselves, get yourselves killed in war. But leave us alone, for we have no need of all these things and we do not wish to participate in acts that are useless as far as we are concerned and above all so evil."

Nothing should be more natural than that the workers should thus express themselves. But part of them, the majority, continue to make martyrs of themselves in the service of the police, in financial offices, in regiments; others, the minority, try to free themselves from oppression by revolt and by committing violence in their turn on those who oppress them, or, in other words, they attempt to quench fire by fire and thus increase the violence from which they are themselves suffering.

Why do men act so irrationally?

It is because the long duration of the lie they suffer from has caused them to lose all notion of the bond that exists between their servitude and their participation in the violence which ensures it.

Why do they not see this bond?

Because they no longer have faith; and without faith men are guided only by self-interest. And he who is guided by self-interest alone cannot do otherwise than deceive or be deceived.

The result is a surprising phenomenon: the masses of the working class, the great majority, continue to support the principle of violence, contrary to common sense and to their own evident interests; in spite of the more and more frequent denunciations of the iniquities from which they are suffering; in spite of revolutions for the purpose of suppressing violence by violence.

All these workers continue out of habit either to profess the false Christian doctrine taught by the Church, or to deny all religion; but they believe in the bottom of their hearts in the ancient law of "a tooth for a tooth," submitting to the detested regime or else seeking to destroy it by violence. The first are powerless to change their situation because, believing in the necessity of the present social organization, they cannot refrain from participating in its violence; the rest, for whom religion has been replaced by political doctrines, cannot free themselves from this violence, because they strive to suppress it by violence of another sort.

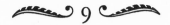 9

The savage instinct of military murder has been so carefully cultivated for thousands of years, that it has become deeply rooted in the human brain. It is to be hoped, however, that a better humanity will know how to free itself from this horrible crime. But what will this better humanity think of the so-called refined civilization of which we are so proud? The same that we think of the ancient inhabitants of Mexico and of their cannibalism—peoples warlike, pious and bestial at the same time.

(Letourneau.)

War will disappear only when men shall take no part whatever in violence and shall be ready to suffer every persecution that their abstention will bring them. It is the only way to abolish war.

(Anatole France. *Daily Reading*, December 29th.)

Ask the majority of Christians what they consider the greatest evil from which Christ freed humanity, and they will answer: from Hell, everlasting fire, and punishment in the next world. And along with this idea, they believe that our salvation may be obtained thanks to the intervention of others. The word Hell, which is seen so seldom in the Scriptures, has done much harm to Christianity as a result of false interpretation. Men flee from an external Hell, when in reality they carry within themselves the Hell that they should fear the most. The salvation that they need is the liberation of their souls from the evil that is concealed within them.

Much worse than any external punishment is the soul in a state of rebellion against God; the soul endowed with

39

divine force yet abandoning itself to bestial passions; the soul living in the sight of God yet fearing the anger of man, preferring glory in other men's eyes to the peaceful realization of its own virtue. There is no greater disaster than this. It is this that impenitent man carries with him to his grave.

To gain salvation in the highest sense of the word, is to lift up the sunken spirit, cure the suffering soul, give it back its liberty of thought, of conscience, of love. In doing this one finds the salvation for which Christ died; it is for this salvation that the Holy Ghost was given to us, it is towards this salvation that the true Christian doctrine is moving.

(Channing.)

It seems so easy to tell the truth; yet it takes a great deal of effort within ourselves to attain this virtue.

A man's degree of veracity indicates the degree of his moral perfection.

(*Daily Reading,* September 19th.)

THE condition of the Christian world indicated in the preceding chapter, as well as that of the rest of the inhabitants of the earth, remains the same as has been described. But I believe that the moment has come, for Russians above all, and for the moujiks in particular, to see at last where lie the means of salvation.

I believe that the Russians are the first to be called to this task because they are less civilized than the other nations; that is to say they are less corrupted intellectually and have kept a vague, but profound understanding of the Christian religion. They are called to-day precisely because they have just gone through a grotesque, pitiful revolution and a repression horrible in its unprecedented insolence and stupid cruelty.

The means of salvation of which I am speaking has been foreseen by men for a long time, but it is only lately that they have been becoming conscious of it and starting to apply it.

A military court is sitting in a Russian provincial town. The judges are seated before a table; on this table is the mirror of justice, surmounted by the two-headed imperial eagle and carrying an inscription on its base; also law books and sheets of paper with headings well laid out.

Among the judges, in the place of honour, is seated a stout man in uniform, with a cross on his collar; he seems rather intelligent, good-natured, even tender hearted because he has lunched well and has received comforting news about his youngest son's health. At his side is another officer of German origin, who is displeased at having been appointed, and is going over in his head the terms of the report that he is about to address to his chief. The third place is occupied by a very young officer, elegant, good-humoured, still thinking of the epigram that he ventured to make while lunching at the colonel's, and which amused the guests so much. He is still smiling about it. He is frantically anxious to smoke, and is impatiently awaiting the end of the session.

At a short distance the clerk of the court is sitting in front of a small table. He is absorbed in inspecting a bundle of papers, among which he will choose the documents to be asked for presently at the first injunction.

Two young people, one a peasant from the government of Panza, the other a petit bourgeois from the town of Lubin, are both dressed as troopers. A third is brought in, dressed like the others and quite young.

This young man is very pale. He casts a rapid glance at the court, then his eyes take on a vague expression. He has passed three years in prison for having refused to take the recruitment oath for military service. In order to get rid of him after three years of prison, he has been offered an opportunity to swear allegiance, after which he could be set at liberty as having served three years although he passed them in prison. But he has again refused, declaring, as he did the first time, that he was a Christian, that he could not possibly swear an oath of allegiance or become a murderer. This is why he has been brought before a court-martial.

The registrar reads a paper called the act of accusation. It is noted that the young man has refused to touch the pay and considers that military service is a sin.

The president good-naturedly asks the accused if he is guilty.

"Everything that has been read is exact: I acted

and spoke like that, but I do not consider myself guilty," answers the young man in a voice trembling with emotion.

The president nods his head in assent, as if the reply was what he expected it to be; he consults a paper and asks:

"What do you say in explanation of your conduct?"

"I have refused and I still refuse because I consider military service a sin ... contrary to the teaching of Christ."

The president, satisfied, nods again in approval: everything is in order.

"Have you anything to add?"

The young man explains with a trembling of the jaw that it is written in the Scriptures that murder is forbidden, and not only murder but any hostile feeling towards one's neighbour.

The president keeps on approving. The German officer frowns; the young officer, head and eyebrows raised, becomes attentive as if he were hearing something new and interesting.

The accused, becoming more and more agitated, says that the oath is positively forbidden, and that he would consider himself guilty if he had consented to serve, that he was again ready ...

This time the president stops him, finding that the accused is digressing and making futile remarks.

The witnesses are called: the colonel of the regiment and the sergeant. The colonel is the president's usual partner at cards and an excellent player. The sergeant is a Pole belonging to the minor nobility, clever, handsome and a great reader of fiction.

Then in comes the priest, a rather elderly man. He has just left his daughter, son-in-law and grandchildren who have come to visit him, and he is still suffering from the effect of a quarrel with his wife on account of a carpet that against her wish he has given to his daughter.

"Father, please swear in the witnesses, and tell them the sin they will commit against God by not telling all the truth," says the president, addressing the priest.

The latter puts on his vestments, takes the cross and the Bible, then pronounces the usual exhortation.

The colonel is the first to take the oath; raising rapidly two very clean fingers, already well known to the president, he repeats after the priest the formula of the oath, and kisses the cross and Bible noisily, as if the act gave him pleasure.

Then it is the turn of the Catholic priest to swear in the handsome sergeant with the same speed.

The judges wait, grave and calm. The young officer, who had gone out for a minute to take a few puffs of a cigarette, comes back during the deposition of the witnesses, who punctually confirm what the accused has said. The president nods approvingly.

After this an officer placed at a certain distance from the judges gets up; he is the counsel for the prosecution. He approaches the desk, takes up the papers lying there, and begins to speak in a loud voice, setting forth in well linked sentences everything that the young man has done, which the judges know already, and which the accused has just admitted, without trying to minimize his crime but rather aggravating it.

The prosecutor states that, according to the young man's own declaration, he does not belong to any sect, that his parents are orthodox, and that to begin with his refusal to serve was pure recalcitrance. This obstinacy, not only of the accused, but of others like him, obliges the government to take the severest measures against them and these are applicable in the present case.

Then it is the turn of the counsel for the defence, who gives out a few thoughts which do not seem to have much connection with the affair.

Then everyone goes out, comes back; the accused is summoned, and the court reconvenes. The judges first sit down, then get up, and the president, without looking at the accused, reads the sentence in a quiet, even voice: the accused, who has already suffered three years for not being a soldier, is condemned: first to be dismissed from the army and deprived of all his rights and privileges; secondly, to four years of prison.

The guard leads out the young man; then all those

who have taken part in the ceremony return to their habitual occupations and distractions, as if nothing in particular had happened.

Except that the young officer, the smoker, feels a strange twinge of uneasiness, which recurs each time he thinks of the strong, noble words of the accused, said with so much emotion. During the deliberations the young officer had a sudden wish to express an opinion contrary to the decision of his elders; but he had been embarrassed, swallowed his saliva and agreed.

That evening, at the home of the colonel of the regiment, when between two games of cards all the guests were seated around the tea table, the conversation drifted round to the case of the rebellious soldier. The colonel expressed his clear opinion that lack of education was the cause of such incidents; one assimilates all kinds of ideas without taking care to adapt them to circumstances, and that leads to all sorts of extravagances.

"Pardon me, uncle," said a student, a social democrat, and the colonel's niece. "The firm opinions and the energy of this man are worthy of respect. One should only regret that this force has taken a wrong direction," added the young girl, thinking how valuable such energies would be if used in the service of socialist ideas, instead of being wasted on out-of-date religious fantasies.

"Come, you are a mad revolutionary," said her uncle, with a smile.

The young officer, cigarette in mouth, intervened in his turn:

"Yet it seems to me that from the Christian point of view it would be difficult to contradict the young man."

"I don't know anything about any point of view," said a general severely. "But I do know that a soldier should be a soldier, and not a preacher."

"In my opinion," said the president of the tribunal, his eyes twinkling. "The most important thing of all is not to lose time if we want to finish our game."

"If any of you want more tea, you will be served at the card table," said the master of the house amiably, while one of the players in a practised manner threw the cards fan-shape on the table. Each one took his place.

In the prison entrance, where the soldiers who were escorting the prisoner were waiting with him for their orders, another conversation took place:

"How is it that the priest does not understand what is said exactly in the books?" asked one of the soldiers in the Ukrainian dialect.

"Naturally he doesn't understand," answered the prisoner. "Or he would have said as I do: Christ commands us to love and not to kill."

"That is true, but very difficult."

"It is not at all difficult. Look at me, I have been locked up, and I am going to be locked up again; but I have such a lightness of heart that I wish you all had the same."

A middle-aged noncommissioned officer drew near, and addressing the prisoner, said to him respectfully:

"Well, Seminitch, you've been condemned?"

"Yes, of course."

The noncommissioned officer shook his head, and added:

"That is all very well, but one has to suffer for it."

"It is necessary," answered the prisoner with a smile, visibly touched by this sympathy.

"I know: Our Lord suffered and He told us to suffer also; but it is difficult, just the same."

As he was speaking, the handsome Polish sergeant entered with a quick, authoritative step, and said briefly:

"No talk here. Take him to prison."

The sergeant was especially severe, because he had received orders to see that the prisoner did not talk with the soldiers. In fact, during the time that this refractory youth had been in prison, four men had already been seduced in this way by him; they had been court-martialled for refusing to serve, and were now imprisoned in their turn.

It is much more natural to conceive of a society directed and guided by rational ideas that are profitable to every one than the society of the present day, where violence alone determines the conduct of men.

It is likely that constraint exercised by the state was necessary in former days to assure the survival of societies; perhaps it is still necessary to-day; but men can no longer close their eyes, or help being aware of a possible state of things in which violence can be only a nuisance in their peaceful existence. It follows that in seeing it, or in feeling it, they cannot prevent themselves from seeking to bring about this order of things. The means of doing that is in the moral improvement of each one of us, and in abstention from all violence.

(*Daily Reading*, October 13th.)

THE declarations made before military judges by conscientious objectors are only repetitions of what has been said since the first appearance of the Christian religion. The most ardent and sincere fathers of the Church declared the teaching of Christ to be incompatible with one of the fundamental conditions of the existence of the State: armed force. In other words a Christian must not be a soldier prepared to kill every one whom he is ordered to.

The Christian communities of the first four centuries declared categorically from the very mouths of their pastors the prohibition of all murder, either individual or else collective—that is, war.

In the second century the philosopher Tatian, a convert to Christianity, considered murder in warfare to be just as inadmissible for his co-religionists as any other kind of assassination, and looked upon the laurel crown of the victor as an unworthy symbol. In the same period Athinagorus of Athens says that not only must Christians not kill, but that they must not be witnesses of assassinations. In the third century Clement of Alexandria contrasted *warlike* pagans with "the peaceful community of Christians."

But it was Origen who most forcibly expressed the Christian's disgust with war. In applying the words of Isaiah to the Christians: the time would come when men would change their swords for sickles and their lances for ploughs, he says clearly: "We do not arm ourselves against any nation; we do not learn the art of war, because through Jesus Christ we have become the children of peace." Answering the accusation of Celsus against Christians who avoided military service (for, in his opinion, the Roman Empire would disappear as soon as it became Christian), Origen said that Christians fought more than the rest for the welfare of the emperor, since they defended him by good actions, by prayers and good influence on other men. As to armed combat, Origen added that certainly they should not take part with the imperial armies not even if the emperor himself obliged them to do so.

Tertullian, a contemporary of Origen, expressed himself no less categorically on the impossibility of Christians being warriors. Speaking of military service he said: "It is not fitting to serve at the same time the symbol of Christ and the symbol of the devil, the power of light, and the power of darkness. One and the same soul cannot serve two masters. And how may we wage war without the sword that God himself has taken away from us? How can we learn the use of the sword, when Our Lord said that he who raised the sword would perish by the sword? And how can the sons of peace take part in combat?"

The celebrated Cyprian in his turn said: "The world is going mad in mutual extermination; and murder, considered as a crime when committed individually, becomes a virtue when it is committed by large numbers. It is the multiplication of their crimes that assures impunity to these assassins."

In the fourth century Lactance declared the same thing: "There cannot be a thousand exceptions to God's commandment: Thou shalt not kill. No arm save truth should be carried by Christians."

The rules of the Church of Egypt in the third century, as well as the Testament of Our Lord Jesus Christ, absolutely forbid any Christian to serve in the army, under pain of excommunication.

In the *Acts of the Saints*, there are many examples of martyrdom suffered by the faithful of Christ for having refused to serve. For example, Maximilian who, brought before the conscription council and asked to give his name to the proconsul, answered: "I am called a Christian, and consequently am not a warrior." He was delivered to the executioner.

Marcellus was a centurion in the Legion of Troy. Having embraced the Christian religion, and being convinced that war was an impious act, he took off his armour before the whole legion, threw it on the ground, and declared that having become a Christian he could no longer remain in the army. He was imprisoned, but again he repeated: "A Christian must not carry arms." He was executed.

Cassius likewise confessed to the same religion and refused to serve. He suffered the same fate.

Under Julian the Apostate, Martin, brought up to be a soldier, refused to continue his service. During the examination that the emperor made him undergo he only answered with these words:

"I am a Christian and therefore am not a warrior."

In the year 325, the first general council instituted a severe penance for Christians who went back to the army after having left it. Here are the exact terms of this order in the Russian translation, recognized by the Orthodox Church.

"Called by grace to the profession of faith and having shown their first ardour in removing their warlike accoutrements, then having returned to them like dogs towards their vomitings . . . they should implore the Church for a period of ten years; asking pardon and listening to the Scriptures for three years on the threshold of the Church."

Christians enrolled for the first time in the army were instructed not to kill their enemies during war. In the fourth century Basil the Great recommended that soldiers who had infringed this rule should not be admitted to the Communion for three years.

One sees that the conviction that war is incompatible with Christianity was current not only during the first three centuries, during which time Christians were persecuted, but even at the moment of their triumph over paganism, when their doctrine was recognized as the State religion.

Ferrucius declared it very clearly and paid for it with his life. He forbade Christians to shed blood, even in a just war and under the orders of Christian sovereigns. In the fourth century Lucifer, Bishop of Calaris, professed that the Christians should defend their greatest possession, faith, not in killing, but in sacrificing their own lives. Paulin, Bishop of Nole, who died in the year 431, threatened eternal torment to those who served Caesar bearing arms.

This is how it was during the first four centuries of Christianity.

But under the reign of Constantine the standards of the Roman Legions were already carrying the cross. And in 416 an order was decreed with the result that pagans were not admitted to the army.

All the soldiers had become Christians; or, in other words, all the Christians had, with a few exceptions, denied Christ.

Since then, and for about fifteen centuries, the simple and evident truth of the incompatibility of Christianity with the committing of any kind of violence, assassination included, has been so hidden from men that generation after generation has succeeded each other, killed, participated in murders and profited from them, while yet professing the doctrine that condemns them.

The crusades were a mockery, and the most horrible crimes were committed in the name of Christianity; so much so that the few people who kept to the true principles of Christianity, not allowing any violence, the Montagnists, Albigeois, etc., were universally despised or persecuted.

But like fire truth little by little consumes all the disguises that hide it. And since the beginning of the last century it has been revealed with increasing brilliance, attracting attention in spite of all attempts to suppress it. It has been manifested on many occasions but most particularly in the beginning of the nineteenth century in Russia. Its manifestations were doubtless many, but their traces have been effaced; a few only are known to us.

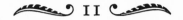 II

*True courage in the struggle cheers the man who knows that
God is his ally.*
  *In the world ye have tribulations: but be of good cheer;
        I have overcome the world.*
                        (John, xvi, 33.)

*Do not wait for the realization of the divine work that you
are serving; but know that not one of your efforts will be
            useless, all will hasten the hour.*
                        (*Daily Reading*, May 24th.)

*The most important acts, both for the one who accomplishes
them and for his fellow creatures, are those that have remote
                    consequences.*
                        (*Daily Reading*, May 28th.)

A governor-in-chief of the Caucasus Mouraviev,
noted the following in his private diary:
  In 1818 five serfs of the Government of Tambov
who has refused to serve in the army were sent to
the Caucasus. On several occasions they were made
to suffer the bastinado, a torture that consisted in
making them pass between two rows of troops, each
soldier in turn striking the victim. But it did no
good. The defaulting recruits repeated: "All men

are equal; our sovereign is a man like us; we will not obey him, we will not pay taxes, and above all, we will not kill men who are our brothers in war. You may cut us up into pieces, we will not yield: we will not wear the uniform, we will not eat at the mess, we will not be soldiers. We will contribute our pennies if you like, but we do not wish to receive any money from the State."

These men and others like them were bastinadoed until they were left for dead; they rotted in prison, and their fate was shrouded in silence. But their number increased nonetheless during the last century.

For example, they say that in 1827 two soldiers of the guard, Nicolaiev and Boddanov, fled into a hermitage of a sect of old believers, installed in the middle of a forest by the merchant Sokolov. When captured, they refused to serve again or to take the oath, because it was contrary to their convictions. The chiefs decided to put them to the torture of the bastinado between two rows of soldiers, and then they were placed in disciplinary companies.

M. Koltchine[1] wrote that: "In 1830, a man and a woman were arrested in the Government of Yaroslav. At their examination the man said that he was named Egor Ivanov, but that he did not know who he was. He had never had any other father, he said, than Christ the Saviour. The woman made the same declaration.

[1] *The Deported and the Prisoners of the Convent of Solovki.*

"During the exhortation made by the priest before the court, the two accused added that they had on earth no other czar than the one in Heaven; that they recognized no emperor, nor any civil or religious authorities. On a second occasion Egor Ivanov, aged seventy-five, repeated that he did not recognize any of the authorities, and that he considered they had all departed from the rules of the Christian religion. He was exiled to the monastery of Solovki to be employed in the works there; but he was shut up, no one knows why, and he remained there until his death. He kept firmly to the position he had taken.

"In 1835 an unknown man calling himself only Ivan was arrested in the Government of Yaroslav. He declared that he did not recognize the saints, the emperor, nor any authority. He was exiled by order of the emperor to Solovki to be employed in the fields. In the same year he was transferred to the army, also by imperial order.

"In 1849 a recruit of the Government of Moscow, Ivan Schouroupov, aged nineteen, refused to take the oath of allegiance, in spite of all the punishments incurred. As the reason for his refusal he gave the Word of God, which commands that God alone shall be served. For this reason he did not wish to serve the emperor or to take the oath of allegiance, for fear of committing perjury. The military authorities, fearing the bad effect that this would have on others, decided to imprison Schouroupov in a monastery without trial. The Emperor Nicholas I inscribed the following resolution on the report of the affair that was presented to him: "Banish the said recruit to the Monastery of Solovki."

Such is the information, recorded in the press, relative to a few isolated cases representing one in a thousand of all those who in Russia have recognized the impossibility of professing Christianity and at the same time obeying the public authorities.

There are also entire communities, counting thousands of members, who are of the same belief; they were very numerous in the last century and still are to-day. I shall mention the Molokanes, Jehovists, Khlisti, Skoptsi, the old believers, and many others, who generally conceal their denial of governmental authority, but consider it as the principle of all evil. It was above all the Doukhobors, who, numbering several tens of thousands, forcibly denied all public authority. Several thousands of these Doukhobors remained firm in their conviction in spite of all the persecutions to which they were exposed. They were finally exiled to Canada.

The number of defaulting recruits increases more and more. From the time that our government instituted universal military service, conscientious objection on the part of true Christians continued to multiply. No persecution, no punishment stops these young people in face of what they consider disobedience to Divine law.

By chance I have known quite a number of these

men who have suffered painfully for their faith in Russia, and many of whom are still detained in prison. Here are the names of some of these victims: Zalubovsky, Lubitch, Mokeïev, Drojjine, Izumtchenko, Olkhovik, Sereda, Farafonov, Egorov, Gancha, Akoulov, Tchaga, Dimchitz, Ivtchenko, Bezverkhi, Slobodnuk, Mironov, Bougaiev, Tchelichev, Menchikov, Reznikov, Rojkov, Chevtchouk, Bourov, Gontcharenka, Zakharov, Tregoubov, Volkov, Koschevoï.

Among those who are imprisoned I know: Ikonnikov, Kourtych, Varnavsky, Chniakine, Molossaï, Koudrine, Pantchikov, Deriabine, Kalatchev, Bannov, Zinkitchev, Martchenko, Prozretsky, Davidov.

I know others in Austria, in Hungary, Serbia, Bulgaria, Holland, France, Switzerland, Sweden, Belgium. Such refusals to serve in the army have also taken place lately and for the same motives in the Muslim world, notably among the Babides, in Persia, and in the sect of the Legion of God in Russia.

The motive for these refusals is always the same, as natural, as necessary and as incontrovertible: the recognition of the necessity of observing the religious rather than the civil law when these are in opposition. And the belief that a civil law exacting military service, that is to say the preparedness to kill by order from above, can only be in opposition to all religious and moral law which is always founded on love of one's neighbour. It is the case

Antigone!

for all religions, for Christianity as well as for Islam, Buddhism, Hinduism and Confucianism.

The definition of the law of love given nineteen centuries ago by Christ has in our days penetrated the consciousness of men, no longer only as a result of the observance of Christ's teaching, but directly, among all those in whom the moral sense is developed.

Here, and only here is our salvation.

It would seem at first sight that these refusals to serve in the army are only isolated cases. But one forgets that these are not occasional and circumstantial acts, but the result of sincerely held religious beliefs.

It is evident, then, that this faith undermines everything based on principles contrary to it; and that in fact as soon as men understand that their participation in violence is incompatible with the Christianity they profess, as soon as they refuse to serve as soldiers, tax collectors, judges, jury, and police agents, the violence from which the whole world suffers will disappear forthwith.

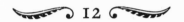

12

When you can say with entire truth and with a whole heart: "Lord God, lead me wherever thou desirest," then and only then do you deliver yourself from servitude and become really free.

(*Thoughts of the Wise*, April 14th.)[1]

A free man is only master of what he can dispose of without hindrance. But one can only dispose entirely of oneself. That is why, when you see that a man wishes to dispose not of himself, but of others, know that he is not free: he has become the slave of his desire to dominate men.

(Epictetus. *Thoughts of the Wise*. June 11th.)

W HAT can these hundreds, these thousands— say if you like, these hundreds of thousands of men—feeble, powerless, isolated, do in the presence of a considerable number of other men, obedient to the orders of governments and provided with the most formidable weapons of destruction? Does not the struggle seem unequal, impossible?

Nevertheless, the result of this struggle is as little in doubt as is the struggle between the shades of night and the light of dawn.

Here is what was written by one of these young

[1] Another collection of Tolstoy, made before *Daily Reading.*

men who was imprisoned for having refused to serve in the army:

"Sometimes I am able to speak with soldiers of the guard, and I cannot help smiling when they say to me:

'Come, my lad, it can't be very easy for you to waste all the years of your youth in prison.'

'Doesn't it all end the same way?' I say.

'That's true, but you wouldn't be so badly off in the regiment, if you wished to serve.'

'I'm better off here than the rest of you in the regiment.'

"And they answer a little ironically:

'That's true. But just the same it's now four years you've been imprisoned, while if you'd done your military service, you'd have been free long ago.'

'But since I'm allright here . . .'

'That's strange,' replies one soldier, shaking his head, and looking pensive.

"I have the same conversations with the soldiers imprisoned with me:

'It's astonishing. You put up with everything, and in spite of all, you're always gay and active,' one of them said to me, a soldier of Jewish origin.

"My prison comrades say when they see any of their number become sad:

'Look here, you're scarcely shut up before you start pining away. Look at Dad (that is what they call me on account of my beard), he's been here for a long time, but he's always gay.'

"And a long conversation follows, sometimes for the sake of talking, but sometimes in order to speak of God, of life, and of other interesting things. Or else one of my comrades speaks of his life in his village, and one feels so well, just listening. In fact, I cannot complain of my existence here."

Another writes:

"I will not say that my mental life is always the same. I pass moments sometimes of lassitude, sometimes of joy.

"At the present time I am feeling well. But just the same it takes a lot of strength to take part in what goes on in prison with a feeling of triumph. In order not to give way, I try to see into the depths of things, and to persuade myself that all this is transitory, that I have more force within me than is needed for whatever the case may be; then joy brightens my heart again, and wipes away everything that has just happened. It is in this interior struggle that my existence continues."

A third writes:

"Sentence has been passed. I am condemned to five years, five months, and six days of prison. You could never believe the joy and peace I felt after the judgment, as if I had been relieved of an enormous weight. I wish I could always feel as light and well."

Quite different is the state of soul of those who participate in violence, submitting to it or profiting by it. All these thousands, all these millions of men are ignorant of the totally natural feeling of love for one's neighbour; on the contrary, they hate, blame, or fear, suppressing all their humane feelings to such a point that the assassination of their brothers seems almost indispensable to their well-being.

"You reproach us for the cruelty of the executions," say the Russian conservatives of to-day. "But what shall we do with these wretches? In France they quieted the country only after cutting off innumerable heads. Let them stop throwing bombs, and we will stop hanging them."

With the same inhuman cruelty revolutionary leaders demand the death of the leaders of the government. The revolutionaries, workmen from the factories or the fields, demand the death of the capitalists and the landed proprietors. These men know that their acts are contrary to human nature and they lie, seeking to arouse wickedness in themselves, in order to smother the truth that is in them, and they suffer from the sharpest evil of all, that of the soul.

Some believe that they are impelled by human nature to accomplish the task towards which all humanity is tending, and which results in certain good, as much to the individual as collectively. Others, in spite of all their efforts to hide it from themselves, know that all their acts are contrary to our nature and that they are keeping to a task from which humanity is constantly withdrawing; as a result of which mankind as a whole is suffering, as well as each one of us individually, and they them-

selves more than any. On one side are liberty, peace
and sincerity; on the other, slavery, fear and dis-
simulation. On the one side is faith, on the other
lack of belief; on one side truth, on the other lies;
on one side love, on the other hatred; on one side
a radiant future, and on the other a frightful past.

How can one doubt which side will be victorious?

What irrefutable truths were expressed by a
French writer, now dead, when he wrote this
marvellously inspired letter:[1]

"No matter what he does, no matter what he says,
no matter what one says to him, man has only one
body to nourish, one intelligence to cultivate and
develop; he has one soul to satisfy. This soul is
working incessantly, in continual evolution towards
light and truth. As long as it has not received all the
light, or conquered all the truth, it will remain a
torment to him.

"It has never tormented him, never oppressed him
as much as to-day. It is, as it were, spread out in the
very air one breathes. The individual souls, who in
isolation have had the desire for social regeneration,
have gradually sought out each other, approached
each other, united and understood each other, and
have formed a group, a centre of attraction towards
which other souls now fly from the four quarters of
the globe, as swallows towards a mirror. They constitute, so to speak, a collective soul, to the end that

---

[1] Letter from A. Dumas fils to the director of the Gaullois,
entitled *Mysticism in School*.

in future men may realize in common, consciously and irresistibly, the common union between nations who have recently been hostile to each other. I find and recognize this new soul in facts that seem the most likely to deny its existence.

"This arming of the nations, the threats their leaders hurl at each other, this renewing of race persecution, these enmities among compatriots, and even the horseplay in the Sorbonne are symptoms that look bad but augur well. They are in fact the last convulsions of what is going to disappear. The social body acts like the human body; the malady is only the violent effort of the organism to free itself from a morbid and harmful element.

"Those who have profited, and who hope to go on profiting for a long time from the errors of the past, will unite in order that nothing shall be changed. As a result, there are these armaments, these threats, these persecutions; but if you look closely you will see that all that is merely external. It is colossal and empty. These millions of armed men, who are exercising every day in preparation for a general war of extermination, do not hate those they must fight, and not one of their chiefs dares to declare this war. As for the demands, even the most serious ones, of those at the bottom, a great and sincere pity which at last recognizes them as legitimate is answering them from above.

"A great coming together is inevitable soon, and sooner than one supposes. I do not know if it is because I am shortly going to leave this world, and if the glimmerings of light beyond the horizon have enlightened me also, affecting my vision, but I believe that our world is soon going to see the realization of the words: 'Love one another,' without preoccupying itself with whether it was a man or a God who said them."

Yes, it is only in the practical realization of the law of love, in its true meaning, that is to say, as a supreme law admitting no exception, in which is to be found the salvation from the horrible condition at present confronting the nations of the Christian world; a condition which is gradually reaching the point of seeming to have no solution.

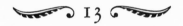

13

Social life can be bettered only by individual self-denial.
(*Daily Reading*, January 19th.)

*Do what you have to do in life according to divine will,
and in that way you will take part in the improvement of
the lives of everybody.*
(*Daily Reading*, January 17th.)

"THE crushing heaviness of evil is weighing down on men," I wrote fifteen years ago. "They are seeking out ways to free themselves from it. They know that by uniting their efforts they would be able to lift up this weight and throw it off; but they cannot agree as to how they shall work together when everyone is sinking lower and lower, leaving the weight heavier on the shoulders of the rest. This weight would have crushed them long ago if men had not been found who thought less of the consequences of their acts than of their accord with the calls of their consciences.

"These men are Christians. They are so because instead of seeking to attain an external goal, for which one must get the co-operation of other people, they see only their internal goal, for the realization of which it is not necessary to depend on any one

69

else; and this is the foundation of true Christianity.

"That is why freedom from the servitude in which we find ourselves at present is impossible for those who seek it in collective effort. It can only be obtained by the substitution of the law of love for the law of violence, that fundamental principle of Christianity.

"This doctrine says to each isolated individual: You cannot know the end of social life; you can only envisage it as a form of progressive approach towards universal happiness, towards the realization of the Kingdom of God on earth. On the other hand, you are aware of the aim of personal life: it is the development in each of the greatest amount of love, in order that the kingdom of God may be established. This aim is certain and is easy to approach.

"You can be ignorant of the best methods for attaining this external goal; you can meet obstacles in the way of its realization; but nothing can stop your drawing nearer to inner perfection: the increase of love in yourself and towards others.

"So it is enough to institute, in the place of this illusory social goal, this individual aim of life, the only sure and accessible one; and the chains you thought were fastening you forever will drop immediately and you will feel yourself absolutely free . . .

"The Christian can ignore the laws established by the State because he has no need of them for himself, or for others; he considers that human life is better assured by the law of love he professes than by the law of violence imposed on him . . .

"Having recognized the efficacy of the law of love, he does not consider the law of violence obligatory, and he denounces it as the most horrible of mistakes. . . .

"The profession of true Christianity which includes the precept of nonresistance to violence and evil relieves the faithful from belief in any external authority. In fact it gives them the chance to achieve those better conditions in life that at present men seek vainly to secure by changing its external forms. It is generally believed that society improves as a result of external changes whereas in reality it changes only with changes in the human conscience, and to the extent that this conscience has evolved.

"It was not the orders of a government that abolished the murder of children, torture and slavery but the general conscience that demanded these orders.

"Since the evolution of conscience determines changes in our social forms, it is argued the contrary should equally well apply; and as it is more agreeable and easier to modify external forms (because the results are more obviously apparent), such course of action is preferred to that whose aim is to change men's consciences. That is why men are more frequently preoccupied not with the foundation, but with the mere forms of life.

"It is often argued in proof of the falsity and impracticality of the Christian ideal the fact that although revealed to men nineteen centuries ago it has been adopted by them only outwardly. It is said that if it has been known for so long and has not become our rule of conduct, if so many Christian martyrs have died without making any change in the order of things, that clearly shows that the ideal itself is false and unattainable.

"To think and speak thus is to say that seeds buried in the earth and not sprouting instantly are not good seeds and should be destroyed.

"It was inevitable that the Christian ideal was not accepted in its full meaning at the moment of its formulation. A doctrine undermining the whole existing order of things could not possibly have been accepted in its entirety; that is why it was adopted only in a misrepresented form. The great majority of men were incapable at that time of assimilating this ideal by spiritual means. They had to be shown first by experience that all departures from the commandments of the Christian doctrine would be disastrous to them.

"The Christian doctrine was therefore accepted as a new exterior cult, replacing paganism, but the pagan conditions of life did not undergo any change whatever. Nevertheless, misrepresented as it was, this doctrine based on the Scripture could not help but produce an effect, which in spite of all the efforts of the servants of false Christianity to hide its true meaning, has penetrated little by little into the consciences of men.

"These two contrary trends, positive and negative, have continued for eighteen centuries. On the one hand people have been drawn further and further away from the possibility of leading reasonable and decent lives; on the other hand the doctrine has been coming to be seen more and more in its true light.

"In our own time we already see true Christianity, until now comprehended by only a few minds endowed with religious feeling, manifested in the form of socialist doctrines, accessible to the simplest, though the forms of social life continue to exist in evident contradiction to this truth.

"One trembles before the present horrible condition of human life: taxes, clergy, great landed properties, prisons, guillotines, cannon, dynamite, millionaires and beggars. In reality all these horrors are the result of our own acts. Not only can they disappear, but they must disappear, in conformity with the new conscience of humanity. Christ said that He had conquered the world; and in fact He has conquered it. Dreadful as it may be, the evil no longer really exists because it is disappearing from the consciences of men.

"To-day humanity is passing through a transitory phase. Everything is ready for passing from one state of the human condition to another; it needs only a slight push to set it off and it can take place at any minute.

"The social conscience of humanity already condemns the former way of life and is ready to adopt the new. The whole world feels it, and is convinced of it. But inertia and fear of the unknown retards the application in practice of what has for a long time been realized in theory. In such cases it sometimes needs only one word to make the force called public opinion change the whole order of things at once, and do it without struggle or violence.

"The freeing of men from servitude, from ignorance, can not be obtained by revolution, syndicates, peace congresses, etc., but simply by the conscience of each one of us forbidding us to participate in violence and asking us in amazement: Why are you doing that?

"It is enough for us to emerge from the hypnosis that hides our true mission from us, for us to ask with dread and indignation how any one can insist upon our committing such horrible crimes. And this awakening can take place at any instant."

This is what I wrote fifteen years ago, and I repeat to-day with conviction that this awakening is about to take place.

Certainly I shall not be there to take part in it. I, an old man, more than eighty years of age; but I know with the same certainty as I see spring follow winter and night day, that this hour has already come in the life of Christian humanity.

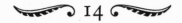 14

The human soul is Christian in its nature. Christianity is always accepted by man as a remembrance of something forgotten. It raises him to a height from which he discovers a world of happiness, ruled by a natural law. Man's feelings on discovering the natural truth are like those of a prisoner who has been confined in a tall dark tower and who, climbing to its highest balcony, discovers a marvellous world, till then unsuspected by him.

The idea of having to submit to man's law is enslaving; the idea of submitting to God's law sets one free.
(*Daily Reading*, January 28th.)

One of the surest conditions of human action is the fact that the further away is the goal towards which we are struggling, and the less we desire to witness the fruit of our efforts, the more certain we are of our success.
(John Ruskin.)

The most important and the most necessary work for its author, as for others, is the one that is only fully appreciated a long time after his death.
(*Daily Reading*, May 28th.)

"IN order for men to be able to get rid of a government founded on violence, they must all be religious; in other words, they must all be prepared to sacrifice their material good to God's law, and live not for the future but for the present, in forcing themselves to accomplish the divine will which is based on love. But the men of our time are not religious and cannot consequently adopt this line of conduct."

Those who say this suppose that to be religious is a state contrary to our nature; that it is manifested only in exceptional cases, and is the effect of education or suggestion. In reality, it is the absence of faith, the only natural condition of life, that causes men to-day to believe that religion is not a natural need.

Just as work is not an artificial thing imposed on men, but something inevitable, without which men cannot live, so faith, that is to say the consciousness of man's relation to the universe and the rule of conduct resulting from it, is an inevitable phenomenon. This faith, far from being artificial, exceptional, inculcated by education, is in human nature; we cannot do without it any more than birds who have lost their wings can fly.

If in the Christian world to-day we see men deprived of conscience, or rather, whose religious feeling has been obscured, this abnormal situation is temporary and fortuitous, bred of the special conditions in which men are now living; this state is as exceptional as that of men who live without working.

So in order to recapture this sentiment which is natural and indispensable to life, it is necessary for men to dissipate the lies that obscure it within them.

It will be sufficient to free them from the deception of the Christian doctrine as corrupted by the Church, which justifies a social organization founded on violence, for the chief obstacle to the supreme law of love to disappear at once; the law that tolerates no exception was revealed to humanity nineteen centuries ago and is the only answer to the demands of our modern conscience.

From the moment that this law penetrates the universal conscience as the *supreme law* of life, our dreadful moral condition which permits the greatest iniquities and acts of barbarism to be considered natural will disappear of itself. Then everything dreamed of and promised to-day by socialist and communist builders of future worlds will come to pass. The result obtained will be even greater than that.

And this end will be attained precisely because it will not be necessary to make use of the violent methods extolled to-day. We will be free from the evil that is torturing and corrupting the whole world, not by preserving the present regimes, monarchies or republics, or by suppressing them and replacing them with socialist or communist ones; or in general, by conceiving of any future regime and trying to impose it by force. But by having recourse to this sole rule: each one of us, without worrying about the result to ourselves or others, must in our own lives observe the supreme law of love condemning every form of violence.

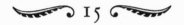

15

A man who continues to live in error sees the incarnation of power in certain institutions which are considered the sacred and indispensable organs of the social body. The man who awakens to the truth sees this power assumed by men swallowed up in error who attribute to it a fantastic importance having no possible intelligent justification, and who accomplish their will by force.

For the clear sighted, these lost people, bribed as often as not, resemble brigands who hold up travellers on high roads. For any one who has awakened to the truth, the entity called a State does not exist, and therefore there does not exist the slightest justification for the acts of violence committed in the name of the State, and so any participation in these acts is impossible for him.

Eventually institutional violence will disappear, not as a result of external action, but thanks only to the calls of conscience of men who have awakened to the truth.

(*Daily Reading*, October 16th.)

T HE objection will be made: "But how can we get along without a government, or any public authority? No state of society has ever existed without one or the other."

Men are so accustomed to the government under which they live that it seems to them an inevitable, permanent form of social life. But it is only so in appearance; men have lived and are still living out-side of any state organization. All primitive peoples who have not yet attained what we call civilization have lived and are still living in this way; also men whose conception of life go beyond it. In Europe, in America, and above all in Russia, there are small Christian communities which deny public authority, not feeling the need of it themselves and submitting only to outside interference when forced to.

The State is only a temporary form of human grouping. Just as the life of an individual can evolve and perfect itself, so the condition of humanity in its entirety progresses and improves.

Every human being begins as an infant, then plays, studies, starts to work, marries, brings up children, rids himself gradually of his passions, and acquires wisdom with old age. The life of nations evolves in the same way; only their phases of development last not years, but centuries and millennia. And in the same way as with the individual the essential trans-formations take place in the spiritual, intangible world, so the essential changes in humanity as a whole take place in the intangible world of the religious conscience. And as with the individual the transformations are so slow that one could not indicate the month, the day or the hour when the child becomes a youth, and the youth an adult, and we cannot always say positively when these changes have already taken place; neither can we indicate the epoch when humanity, or a certain part of humanity, has passed from one religious age into another. But as we can perceive that a youth is no longer a child, so we can see that humanity, or a certain part of it, has passed from one epoch into another, when that line has already been crossed.

To-day among the nations of the Christian world we are witnessing the passage of humanity from one age to another.

We do not know the hour when a child becomes a youth, but we know when he can no longer play childish games. We cannot indicate the year, nor even the decade, when the Christian world will pass from its earlier form of life to one determined by religious conscience. But we cannot help seeing that the Christian world can no longer play seriously at military conquest, diplomatic artifice, constitutional devices or at party politics, whether democratic, socialist, revolutionary or anarchist. It can no longer indulge in all those games based on the principle of violence.

This is becoming evident among us particularly in Russia after the external transformation of our political institutions. Serious minded people cannot help feeling towards this new form of government as an adult would feel if he were given a present of a toy that he had never seen as a child. No matter how interesting and new the toy may be, the adult has no need of it and can only accept it with a smile. That is the attitude in Russia of all thinking men as well as of the popular masses in regard to the Constitution, the Douma, and the various parties, revolutionary and otherwise.

The Russians, who I am convinced divine the true sense of Christ's doctrine, can no longer seriously believe that man's mission here below is to employ the short period between his birth and death in making speeches to legislative assemblies, in judging his brothers in the courts, in capturing, imprisoning and assassinating them, or throwing bombs at them or taking away their land; or in bothering as to whether Finland, India, Poland, Korea, are annexed to what is called Russia, England, Prussia or Japan; or in seeking to liberate these annexed countries by force and being prepared to slaughter each other en masse for this purpose. It is impossible for a man of our time to be ignorant in his inner consciousness of the madness of such acts.

For if we do not perceive the horror of the existence we lead, so contrary to our real nature, it is only because the atrocities we tolerate with such equanimity have come upon us so gradually that we do not notice them.

I once saw an old man reduced to a horrible condition: worms were swarming all over his body; he could not move a limb without suffering atrociously. But the progress of the disease had been so slow that he did not notice the horror of it; all he asked for was tea and sugar.

The same with the condition of our society: we

no longer see its horror, because we have come to it by such small degrees, and, as with the old man, we rejoice at the apparition of our cinemas and motor cars.

It is not enough to say that the suppression of violence, violence so contrary to the reasonable and loving nature of man, cannot make our present condition worse; our present condition is so lamentable that it cannot be worse. That is why the question as to whether we can live without governments is not only not gratuitous, as the defenders of the order of existing things would have us believe, but is as ridiculous as it would be to ask a man suffering torture how he would be able to live if his martyrdom was stopped.

The privileged members of our present regime imagine that the absence of all state organization would result in complete anarchy, the struggle of all against all, as if it was a matter of the communal life not of mere animals (they live together in peace without institutional violence) but of I do not know what monstrous creatures, motivated solely by hate and madness. They imagine men to be like this because they attribute to them a disposition contrary to their nature and which in reality is developed by the very regime they perpetuate, in spite of all the evil that it causes to mankind.

The question as to what life would be like without government, without public authority, can only therefore be answered in this way: it is certain that whatever happens the evils caused by government will disappear: there will be no more exclusive possession of land, no more taxes employed for harmful purposes, no more divisions between nations, or subjection of some by others, no more dissipation of human energy in making war, no more fear of bombs on one side, or of gallows on the other; no more unrestrained luxury for the minority and atrocious poverty for the rest.

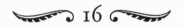

16

We are living in a period of discipline, of culture and of civilization, but it is still far from being a moral one. It could be said that in the present condition of humanity the prosperity of the State increases with the misery of its inhabitants. And one might well ask if we would not be happier living in a primitive condition, deprived of all our present culture. For how can one make men happy without making them moral and good?

(Kant. *Daily Reading*, June 16th.)

Try to conduct yourself in such a way that you have no need to resort to violence.

(*Daily Reading*, October 13th.)

We are well accustomed to reasoning out ways of managing other people's lives; and these reasonings do not seem odd to us.

They would however be superfluous if men were religious and thus free. They are in fact the result of despotism, of the domination of one or of a few over the many.

Not only has one man no right to dispose of a great number, but the great number have no more right to dispose of a single man.

(V. Tchertkov. *Daily Reading*, November 22nd.)

" ALL very wonderful. But will you kindly tell us what form human society will take when it decides to dispense with government?" This is asked by all those who believe that men can always know what our future social life will be, and who therefore expect the same knowledge from those who wish to live without government.

This idea is only a foolish prejudice, very old and widespread as it may be. Men, whether they submit or refuse to submit to governmental authority, never know and can never know what form this future state will take. With even greater reason then would it be impossible for a minority to organize the lives of everybody, for this organization can be effected not according to the will of a few people, but as the result of numerous intervening factors, the principal among which is the religious development of the majority.

The prejudice that causes one to think that he can tell in advance how society will be organized in the future has its origin in the desire of the transgressors to justify their conduct and in the desire of the victims to explain and lighten the weight of their constraint. The former persuade themselves and others that they know the way to make life take the form they consider best. The latter, who undergo such constraint that they do not feel strong enough to free themselves from it, have the same conviction; for it enables them to find some meaning in the situation they suffer.

The Law of Violence

History ought to have destroyed this prejudice entirely, one would have thought.

At the end of the eighteenth century a few Frenchmen tried to maintain the old despotism, but in spite of all their efforts this regime fell, and the republic replaced it. In the same way, in spite of all the efforts of the republican leaders, in spite of all their acts of violence, the empire replaced the republic, and so there followed: empire, coalition, Charles X, a new revolution, a new republic, Louis-Philippe, then various other regimes up to the republic of the present day.

The same facts have been repeated wherever violence has been the basis of action. So, for example, all the efforts of the papacy far from suppressing protestantism have only developed it. And all the efforts of the capitalists have only promoted the cause of socialism.

In sum, even where a regime established by the aid of violence maintains itself for a certain length of time, or changes itself by the use of force, it is only because at that period the form of its social organization continues or ceases to answer to the moral condition of the people. Not because any external cause assures or modifies its existence.

It follows that the axiom whereby a minority can organize the life of the majority, an axiom in the name of which the greatest crimes are committed, is only a fallacy. In the same way the activity that results from it and which is generally considered as most honourable and important, as much by our rulers as by our revolutionaries, is in reality only a pastime as useless as it is harmful, whose chief result is to prevent the realization of the true happiness of humanity.

This fallacy has caused and still causes torrents of blood to flow and the suffering of terrible atrocities. The worst of it is that it has always prevented and still prevents social betterment in conformity with the development of the human conscience. It prevents true progress, because men spend their entire efforts in concerning themselves with others, thereby neglecting their own moral regeneration which alone can effect the regeneration of the world in general.

In fact social life advances, and advances inevitably towards the eternal ideal of perfection, thanks to the progress of individual people on their own paths of perfection, equally unbounded.

One sees from all this the damaging effect of the prejudice that makes us neglect our task of individual betterment which alone procures personal happiness and general welfare. This is the only means really within our power, as opposed to this prejudice that invites us to concern ourselves with the happiness of others—which is not within our power—and makes us employ means of constraint as harmful for ourselves as for others, taking us even further away from individual as well as social perfection.

17

Let each of us concern ourselves only with the solution of the inner question, that of our own conduct in life, and all questions concerning the outer world will receive as a direct result their best possible solution.

We do not know, we cannot know, of what the general good consists; but we do know with certainty that its realization is possible only when we fulfil the law of kindness revealed to each one of us.

If, instead of dreaming of universal salvation we concern ourselves with our own, instead of liberating humanity we liberate ourselves, we would do a great deal more for the salvation and freedom of everyone.
(Herzen. *Daily Reading*, June 30th.)

In individual life and in social life there is only one law: if you wish to better your life, be ready to sacrifice it.
(*Daily Reading*, January 19th.)

Accomplish your task in life by obeying the divine will, and you will then be certain of helping towards the betterment of social life in the most efficient way possible.
(*Daily Reading*, January 17th.)

THE following objection is often made: "All that you say may be true, but it will only be possible to abstain from all violence when the whole world, or at least the majority, will understand its disastrous, futile, and senseless character. While waiting for that, what can a few isolated individuals do? Are we not allowed to defend ourselves, and must we let our neighbours be attacked by the wicked?"

Let us suppose that a brigand is raising his knife over his victim. I see him and am armed with a revolver; so I can kill him. But I am not absolutely certain what the brigand will do. He might not strike; while I would surely kill him. That is why the only thing a man can do in such a case, as in all other similar cases, is to follow an invariable rule of conduct dictated by his conscience. And his conscience may demand of him his own life, but not that of another person.

So to the question as to what one should do in the face of a crime committed by one or by a great number, every man who is free of the idea that it is possible to foresee the future, will answer: Do unto others as you would have them do unto you.

"But others steal, pillage, kill, while I do none of these things. Let them follow the law of mutual help then I in my turn can be asked to observe it." So object our men of the world, with the greater assurance the higher their place in the social scale.

"I do not steal," say the sovereign, the minister, the general, the judge, the landed proprietor, the merchant, the soldier, the police agent. But in fact the idea we have of our social organization, founded on violence, is so impressed upon us that we do not perceive all the crimes committed each day in the name of the public good; we see only the rare attempts at violence of those who are *called* murderers, burglars, or thieves.

"He is a murderer, he is a thief. He does not observe the rule of not doing unto others what you would not have them do unto you," say the same people who do not stop killing others in war, forcing whole nations to prepare for carnage, and who steal from and pillage their own as well as foreign countries. If the rule of mutual help has no more effect upon those who in our society are called murderers or thieves, it is only because they constitute a part of the immense majority of people who for generation upon generation have been robbed and despoiled by men who do not see the criminal character of their own acts.

That is why to the question of knowing what attitude to take towards those who use force against us, one can only answer: "Stop doing unto others what you would not have them do unto you."

Without speaking of the inconsistency and injustice of the punishment in certain cases of violence (when the most horrible crimes committed by the state in the name of the general good are left unpunished), these same punishments have a result actually contrary to what is intended. In effect, they destroy the powerful force of public opinion, which is a hundred times more capable of guaranteeing society against violence than prisons and guillotines.

This reasoning can be applied with striking proof in international relations:—

"How could we do otherwise than resist the invasion of our country by savages who come to take away our property, our wives and daughters?" object those who wish to protect themselves from the same crimes that they commit against other nations. "Yellow peril," shout out the whites; "White peril," cry, with more reason, the Indians, Chinese and Japanese.

But as soon as one is freed from the superstitions that attempt to justify violence, one understands all the horror of the crimes committed by one nation against another; and even more, the moral stupidity that allows the English, Russians, Germans, French, Americans to dream of protecting themselves against the very acts of violence that they commit in India, in Poland, in Manchuria, in Indo China, in Algeria.

It is enough then to free ourselves even for a time from the horrible superstition that lets us believe in the possibility of knowing the future forms of our society (guesswork used to justify every act of violence and lend approval to our present existence) in order to understand immediately that *believing in the need to oppose evil by violence is merely to provide justification for our habitual vices—of vengeance, cupidity, envy, ambition, pride, cowardice, and spite.*

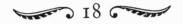

18

The Creator Himself has so arranged matters that human actions must be guided not by interest but by justice; which is why all our efforts to establish the value of such and such interests are in vain. Not one of us has ever known, does not know and can ever know what the result of these actions or series of actions will be for ourselves or for others. But we all can know which action is just, and which is not. We can know also that the consequences of justice will in the end be as good as is possible, for others as for ourselves, although we can never say of what this good will consist.

(John Ruskin.)

And ye shall know the truth, and the truth shall make you free.

(John, viii, 32.)

Man thinks; he was created so. And he should reason in an intelligent way, that is evident. The man who reasons intelligently thinks first of the purpose of his life: thinks of his soul, of God. Now see what men of the world are thinking. Of everything, except that. They dream of danc-ing, music, singing, other pleasures; they are preoccupied in building, getting rich, becoming powerful. They long for riches, they envy kings, and they never think of the mission of humanity.

(Pascal. *Daily Reading,* June 20th.)

FROM the moment that you are liberated, all of you, rulers and rich, oppressed and poor, who suffer from the lies of false and institutional Christianity, lies that hide what Christ revealed to you and what your reason and your heart command, you will understand that the cause of all your physical and moral sufferings has been within yourselves.

Understand then, all of you, that you were born neither slaves nor masters; that you are all free but only so when you observe the supreme law of life and this law is fully revealed to you. It will be sufficient to renounce the lies that hide it from you for you to see at once in what it consists and where your happiness lies. This law is love, and happiness is found in its observance. Understand that, and you will become really free; you will acquire everything you are now vainly seeking to obtain by all the complicated means suggested to you by corrupted men.

> "Come unto me, all ye that labour and are heavy laden, and I will give you rest. Take my yoke upon you, and learn of me; for I am meek and lowly in heart: and ye shall find rest unto your souls. For my yoke is easy and my burden is light."
>
> (Matthew, xi, 28–32.)

You will be preserved from evil and you will obtain what is really good, not by looking after your own interest, not by envy, hatred, anger, ambition; not even by a sense of justice, nor above all by an anxiety for organizing the lives of others; but, strange as it may seem, only by the work of your own soul, not following any outside aim, nor in trying to work out what will come of it.

Understand then that the belief in the possibility of ordering the lives of others is a vulgar prejudice which continues to survive only on account of its antiquity. Understand that the men who make use of it, beginning with the heads of state and their ministers, and ending with the spies and executioners on the one hand, and the leaders and members of the opposition parties on the other, are only pitiable, misled people, occupied with a task not only vain and stupid, but the most abominable that one can conceive of.

Men already see the vileness of the spy and the executioner, and are beginning to see that of the police, police agents, and even to a certain degree, of the military; but they do not yet see that of the judge, the minister, the sovereign, the leaders of political parties and of revolutions. And yet the work of these people is also vile, also contrary to human nature, and even worse than the work of the executioner or the spy because it is more hypocritical.

Understand then, all of you, especially the young, that to want to impose on others by violent means a regime that you can only imagine is not only grossly ignorant but even criminal. Understand that such work, far from assuring the well-being of humanity is only a lie, a more or less unconscious hypocrisy, camouflaging the lowest passions we possess.

Understand it, you, men of tomorrow, and stop looking for an illusionary happiness by participating in the administration of the state, in judicial institutions, in propaganda, in all kinds of political parties whose supposed goal is the good of the masses. Pay attention to only one thing, which we need most, which is the most accessible, which gives the most happiness to ourselves and to every one else: the increase of love in us by the suppression of vicious passions that keep it from manifesting itself. Understand that the observance of this supreme law of love is becoming as inevitable for us as is the law of flight for birds, the law of grazing for the herbiverous, of meat eating for the carnivorous; and that consequently the least transgression of this law is disastrous to us.

Remember it, consecrate your life to this glad work; merely begin and you will see that it is our real work in life, which alone can determine the improvement of our condition—an end that you at present pursue vainly by false means. Do not forget that what we all want in common is the union of men, and that this union can never be attained by means of violence. It is enough that everyone should observe the law of love, and this union will then be realized without the need to seek for it. This *supreme law*, alone, is the same for all of us and unites us all.

Revealed by Christ, it is recognized to-day by

men, and its observance is obligatory as long as there is revealed to us no other law, a still clearer one, conforming better to the calls of the human conscience.

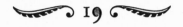

19

Some seek good or happiness in power, others in science,
still others in pleasure. As to those who really understand
what their happiness is, they know that it need not be
possessed by the few but by everyone; they know that the
true good is that which is the lot of all men at the same
time without division or jealousy; no one can lose it except
he who wants to.
(Pascal. *Thoughts of the Wise*, xxvii, 4.)

We possess a single infallible guide and this is the Universal
Spirit that lives in men as a whole, and in each one of us,
which makes us aspire to what we should aspire; it is the
spirit that commands the tree to grow towards the sun,
the flower to throw off its seed in autumn, and us to reach
out towards God and by so doing become united to each other.
(*Daily Reading*, November 16th.)

Salvation lies not in the cult nor in the practice of a religion,
but in the clear comprehension of the meaning of our life.
(*Daily Reading*, September 11th.)

THAT is all I wanted to say.
I wanted to say that we live in a time and are
in a situation in which we can no longer remain, and
from which willingly or not we are obliged to start
out on a new path. And to follow it we do not have
to invent a new religion, or any scientific theories

explaining the meaning of life and serving as a guide to it; it would be futile above all to resort to any special kind of action. It is sufficient simply to adopt this single rule: free ourselves from the superstitions of false Christianity and Statism.

Let each one understand that he has not the right nor even the possibility of organizing the lives of others, but that he in his own life should act only in conformity with the supreme religious law that has been revealed to him. Then the order of things that reigns among the so-called Christian nations—an order that makes the whole world suffer, which answers so little to the demands of our consciences and which makes humanity unhappier each day—will immediately disappear.

Whoever you are: sovereign, judge, proprietor, worker, beggar, reflect and take pity on your soul. No matter how obscured your brain may be by your power, your authority, your wealth, no matter how badly treated and angered you may be by the misery and humiliations you suffer, you possess and you manifest like all of us the divine spirit, which asks you clearly to-day: Why do you make martyrs of yourself and all those about you unhappy? Understand who you are, just how insignificant and infallible is that self which you call "you," which you recognize as your body, and how incommensurable is that which is really you—your spiritual self. Having understood it, begin to live each moment for the accomplishment of your life's purpose which has been revealed to you by universal wisdom, the doctrine of Christ and your own conscience.

Put the good of your life in the progressive liberation of your mind, freedom from all the illusions of the flesh, and in the perfecting of your love for your fellow man—which is in essence the same thing. As soon as you begin to live like this, you will feel a joyous sensation full of liberty and happiness. You will be surprised to find that the same external conditions which caused you such anxiety and which were far from what you wanted will not prevent your experiencing the greatest possible happiness.

And if you are unhappy—I know that you are—reflect upon what has been proposed to you here, which is not the product of my imagination merely but of the thoughts and feelings of the best minds and hearts. It provides the only way to deliver you from your unhappiness and give you the greatest good you can get in this life.

That is what I have wanted to say to you, my brothers. Before I died.